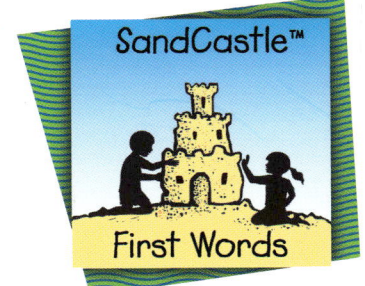

We Look at Food

Mary Elizabeth Salzmann

Consulting Editor, Diane Craig, M.A./Reading Specialist

Published by ABDO Publishing Company, 4940 Viking Drive, Edina, Minnesota 55435.

Copyright © 2006 by Abdo Consulting Group, Inc. International copyrights reserved in all countries. No part of this book may be reproduced in any form without written permission from the publisher. SandCastle™ is a trademark and logo of ABDO Publishing Company.

Printed in the United States.

Credits
Edited by: Pam Price
Curriculum Coordinator: Nancy Tuminelly
Cover and Interior Design and Production: Mighty Media
Photo Credits: AbleStock, BananaStock Ltd., Brand X Pictures, Comstock, Photodisc, Wewerka Photography

Library of Congress Cataloging-in-Publication Data

Salzmann, Mary Elizabeth, 1968-
   We look at food / Mary Elizabeth Salzmann.
      p. cm. -- (First words)
   Includes index.
   ISBN 1-59679-436-4 (hardcover)
   ISBN 1-59679-437-2 (paperback)
      1. Vocabulary--Juvenile literature. I. Title. II. First words (ABDO Publishing Company)
PE1449.S2837 2005
428.1--dc22

                                                              2005043401

SandCastle™ books are created by a professional team of educators, reading specialists, and content developers around five essential components that include phonemic awareness, phonics, vocabulary, text comprehension, and fluency. All books are written, reviewed, and leveled for guided reading, early intervention reading, and Accelerated Reader® programs and designed for use in shared, guided, and independent reading and writing activities to support a balanced approach to literacy instruction.

Let Us Know

After reading the book, SandCastle would like you to tell us your stories about reading. What is your favorite page? Was there something hard that you needed help with? Share the ups and downs of learning to read. We want to hear from you! To get posted on the ABDO Publishing Company Web site, send us e-mail at:

sandcastle@abdopub.com

SandCastle Level: Emerging

About This Series

The *First Words* series provides emerging readers with multiple opportunities to practice reading high-frequency words used in simple text. These books are appropriate for independent, shared, and guided reading.

Red Rebus Section (pages 4–11) Each spread features a predictable, repetitive rebus sentence with a familiar picture clue placed opposite a full-page photograph that strongly supports the text.

Blue Story Section (pages 12–17) An illustrated short story containing the featured sight words offers contextual, repetitive reading opportunities using simple text and familiar letter-sound correspondence.

Green Game Section (pages 18–21) A fun, read-together guessing game based upon the contents of the book expands vocabulary and increases comprehension.

Rebus Glossary (page 22) This list pairs the words and picture clues featured in the rebus sentences.

SandCastle First Thirty Sight Words List (page 23) Use this list to build phonics and word recognition strategies for emerging and beginning readers.

Sight Word Focus

at   look   we

We look at .

We look at .

We look at .

We look at .

We Look at Food

We look at popcorn.

We look at hot dogs.

We look at food.

Look at me!

I am pink and green.

I have seeds.

I am a fruit.

What am I?

I am a watermelon!

Rebus Glossary

hot dogs

popcorn

salad

watermelon

SandCastle First Thirty Sight Words

a	here	not
am	I	on
and	in	said
are	is	see
at	it	the
big	like	this
can	little	to
come	look	up
for	me	we
go	my	you

About SandCastle™

A professional team of educators, reading specialists, and content developers created the SandCastle™ series to support young readers as they develop reading skills and strategies and increase their general knowledge. The SandCastle™ series has four levels that correspond to early literacy development in young children. The levels are provided to help teachers and parents select the appropriate books for young readers.

Emerging Readers
(no flags)

Beginning Readers
(1 flag)

Transitional Readers
(2 flags)

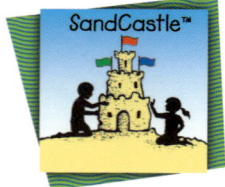

Fluent Readers
(3 flags)

These levels are meant only as a guide. All levels are subject to change.

To see a complete list of SandCastle™ books and other nonfiction titles from ABDO Publishing Company, visit **www.abdopub.com** or contact us at:
4940 Viking Drive, Edina, Minnesota 55435 • 1-800-800-1312 • fax: 1-952-831-1632